Robert Dodge

Tracts for the War

Secession: The Remedy and Result

Robert Dodge

Tracts for the War
Secession: The Remedy and Result

ISBN/EAN: 9783337133535

Printed in Europe, USA, Canada, Australia, Japan

Cover: Foto ©ninafisch / pixelio.de

More available books at **www.hansebooks.com**

𝔄 𝔅𝔬𝔬𝔨 𝔣𝔬𝔯 𝔢𝔳𝔢𝔯𝔶 𝔖𝔬𝔩𝔡𝔦𝔢𝔯'𝔰 𝔎𝔫𝔞𝔭𝔰𝔞𝔠𝔨.

TRACTS FOR THE WAR.

SECESSION:

THE REMEDY AND RESULT.

NEW YORK:
PUBLISHED BY JAMES MILLER,
(SUCCESSOR TO O. S. FRANCIS & CO.)
522 BROADWAY.
1861.

ADVERTISEMENT.

THREE of the within Tracts for the War, entitled Question of the Day, were first printed on their dates, in the *Dispatch*, a newspaper published at Washington, North Carolina, and have been since copied in other newspapers in this country and Europe. The residue have not before appeared. This little volume is designed to put in a more permanent and succinct form, accessible to all, a thorough discussion of the causes and result of secession and the present civil war.

NEW YORK, *May*, 1861.

TRACTS FOR THE WAR.

I.

THE QUESTION OF THE DAY.

THE people of the Northern States have not yet spoken on the grave issues of the day ; and many of us believe that a large proportion of the sober, conservative, law-abiding and patriotic citizens of the South are as yet held in forced silence.

The conduct of some of the present leaders of the South in the seceding States, has shocked the moral sense of the North. The strong phalanx who opposed Lincoln and his party and abolition, with its cry of dissolution of the Union and destruction of the slave power, never believed that the South would be so prompt to attempt such political suicide, and obey the clamors of such fanatics as the abolitionists—their mortal foes. We have been incredulous—have even doubted the verity or earnestness of their acts ; but of several of the States we have ceased to doubt, and have only to deplore that our day should witness such shameless degeneracy in the children of the Father of his Country.

Without other comment, farther than to say that whilst the whole people of the North, East, and West, conscious of their vast predominance, are united in making every reasonable effort in forbearing magnanimity to conciliate and adjust all differences, they are none the less united in the patriotic purpose that, should all such efforts fail, as one man to obey the letter and spirit of the Constitution.

This is the simple and obvious duty, we believe, of every patriotic American ; and without it there can be no government. We are often taunted by the assertion that no power exists in the Constitution to coerce a State ;

that each State is a sovereign, and can secede or rescind the obligations of the Constitution at pleasure ; and when a State has formally seceded, all its citizens are *ipso facto* out of the Union ! released from all obligations for the past or future, and there is no longer any Union or Federal Government, or, we may say, Constitution whatever. Under such pretences they claim absolute impunity and full recognition as independent sovereignties at home and abroad. Let us briefly examine these pretensions by the light of history and reason ; they are fundamental ; the question is worthy of more serious inquiry than may be given it in merely political declamation. Our discussion shall be brief :

" The Articles of Confederation and perpetual union between the States " of 1778 provided by its second article : " That each State retains its sovereignty, freedom, and independence," &c. ; and all its following articles creating a Congress and investing it with executive, judicial, and legislative power, were rendered nugatory, by depriving this body of all power of enforcing its resolves. These articles were created by the States as sovereign States, who acted in Congress through the Revolution *only as States.* It was simply a league or alliance for the common protection, formed by independent States.

Without reciting the familiar history of its inefficiency in the revolutionary struggle, we recur to this old Confederation to fix the fact indelibly in our history, that this Confederation, or former Union, was the *first* and *last* attempt of the States, *as States,* to form a Union. The dogma of complete State sovereignty was then found to be *suicidal* to any Union formed simply *between States.* How could it exist in a Union formed by *all the people residing in the several States ?*

After the peace in 1786, 16th October, Virginia, in the Act of her Assembly providing for the election of delegates to a convention to form a Constitution, in its preamble has this language : " And whereas the General Assembly, taking into view the actual situation of the Confederacy, as well as reflecting on the alarming representations made from time to time by the United States in Congress, particularly in their act of the 15th day of February last, *can no longer doubt that the crisis is arrived* at which the good *people* of America are to decide the solemn question, whether they will, by wise and magnanimous efforts, reap the just fruits of that independence which they have so gloriously acquired, and of that Union which they have cemented with so much of their common blood, or whether, by giving way to unmanly jealousies and prejudices, or to partial and transitory interests, they will renounce the auspicious blessings prepared for them by the Revolution, and furnish to its enemies an eventual triumph over those by whose virtue and valor it has been accomplished ; and whereas the same noble and extended policy, and the same fraternal and affectionate sentiments which originally determined the citizens of this Commonwealth to unite with their brethren of the other States in establishing a Federal Government, cannot but be felt with equal force now, as motives to lay aside every inferior consideration and to concur in such further concessions and provisions as may be necessary to secure the great object for which that government was instituted, and to render the United States as happy in peace as they have been glorious in war ;

Be it enacted, &c., That seven commissioners be appointed by joint ballot to meet such deputies from other States at Philadelphia, and to join with them in "devising and discussing all such alterations and farther provisions as may be necessary to render the Federal Constitution adequate to the exigencies of the Union."

By virtue of this act, Washington, Patrick Henry, Randolph, Madison, and others, were elected Commissioners. We scarcely need an apology for reciting at length the prophetic language of the preamble to this Act of a people, by her recent election, still true to her principles.

The Continental Congress, by its Act of 15th February, 1786, embodying a lengthened report of the utter impossibility of collecting revenue, or sustaining a central government under the Confederation, made dependent on the sovereign will of each State, closed with the Resolution :

"That whilst Congress are denied the means of satisfying those engagements which they have constitutionally entered into for the common benefit of the Union, they hold it to be their duty to warn their constituents" (the States) "that the most fatal evils will inevitably flow from a breach of public faith pledged by solemn contract, and a violation of those principles of justice which are the only solil basis of the honor and prosperity of the nation."

This is an emphatic commentary on the doctrine of *complete State sovereignty*, and on the practical results of mere confederation of independent States, as States.

The Old North State, true to her patriot sires and history, followed Virginia, by her Act of 6th January, 1787, for the election, by joint ballot, of five commissioners to meet at Philadelphia on the 1st of May next, with such

2

deputies from other States, and with them "to discuss and decide upon the most effectual means to remove the defects of our Federal Union, and to procure the enlarged purposes which it was intended to effect :" Whereby Alexander Martin, William Blount, William Richardson Davie, Richard Dobbs Spaight, and Willie Jones, were elected such Deputies.

This paper has already, perhaps, exceeded its just limits. In our next we will pursue our subject.

RODOLPHUS.

February 20, 1861.

II.

THE QUESTION OF THE DAY.

THE Constitution of the United States, framed by the Convention of 1787, called pursuant to the recommendation of the Congress of the Confederation, was submitted to that Congress on 25th September, 1787, and by their resolution transmitted to the Legislatures of the several States, in order to be submitted to a convention of delegates, chosen in each State by the people thereof, in conformity to the resolves of the Convention. It was ratified by the people, who, in January ensuing, chose their first presidential electors, and commenced the government on the first Wednesday (4th) of March, 1789.

The Constitution, in its opening, is expressed to be the *exclusive creation of the People of the United States*, in order to form a *more perfect Union in direct opposition* to the former Confederation.

The States—as States—are *not* parties to the Constitution. But the *whole people in all the States ordain* and *establish* this Constitution of a new Federal Government, *paramount* to all the State Governments, whose *subordinate* existence is recognized therein, and thereby, directly from the people, invest this Federal Government with *supreme* and *exclusive* powers in appropriate spheres.

There is not a word in the instrument recognizing complete State sovereignty, or that this Union and Constitution is an alliance or Confederation of independent States, acting in its ratification or creation by their several agents.

The familiar history of the times shows that such political heresies were universally felt to be the very cardinal evils of the old Confederation, to be remedied by the Constitution.

If, then, the States—as such—never formed this Union under the Constitution, is not the resolve of any State to secede entirely *nugatory*?

The Constitution, in its preamble, ordained and established by the whole people, in its 7th Article, provides that the ratifications of ", the conventions (of the people) of nine States shall be sufficient for the *establishment* of this Constitution between the States *so* ratifying the same."

This organic ordinance of the people was thereby made supreme over all State governments. It was *"ordained"* and *"established,"* in its own emphatic language, and provided the mode of its own amendment ; and also, that this Constitution and the *laws " of the United States,* which shall be made in pursuance thereof, with all treaties, shall be the *supreme law* of the *land,* and the judges in every State shall be bound thereby, *any thing* in the *Constitution* or *Laws* of any State *to the contrary notwithstanding."*

The Federal Government, created by the
2*

Constitution, assumed all debts contracted before the adoption of the Constitution, and was invested with the power to lay and collect taxes and duties, to pay the debts and provide for the common defence and general welfare—to borrow money, regulate foreign commerce, coin money, and fix the standards of value and of weight—to establish post-offices and post-roads, create judicial tribunals, declare war, raise and support armies and navy, and make rules for their government, and call forth the militia to execute the laws of the Union, suppress insurrection, and repel invasions, &c., &c., *and to make* and *enforce all laws* necessary and proper for carrying into effect *all their powers over all the people residing within the United States.*

This supreme Federal Government is, by the laws of Congress and of every State, acknowledged as supreme by the oath of office sworn to by every office-holder in the country, who, if of a State office, thereby swears first above all, to support this Constitution, and next, that of his State, and to perform his duty ; and if of a federal office, swears his allegiance to this Federal Government. With such constant oath-taking—the highest and most solemn sanction on the conscience that man or God imposes—can any one at this day doubt of the supremacy of this Federal Government and the sacred obligation of every citizen to sustain it ?

And, on the other hand, what shall be said of those citizens, many of them high in rank in the army and navy, and holding civil and judicial offices of trust and distinction under the Constitution, who, pretending that their allegiance to their native States is superior, openly break their official oaths and join the declared enemies of the Constitution and the Union, by which, in many cases, for all their lives, they have been educated and maintained out of the Federal treasury ? We use plain language at the North, and adopt the words of the Constitution in calling them traitors—recreants to their oaths and country, and deplore their contrast with the conduct of Major Anderson.

Another question is immediately involved :
Is not this Federal Constitution of government
of perpetual obligation on every citizen ?   It
is so by the definition of the powers vested in
it by the people.   Unless this Government be
perpetual and supreme, all treaties are dissolved, and all laws and contracts by the Federal
Government, disposing, as they constitutionally
have forever, of vast territorial and other property, for over seventy years past, must be re-
scinded, and the nation justly execrated by all
civilized Governments, for setting up a gov-
ernmental mockery to be repudiated on any
caprice.   Such a result is immediate and inevitable to the opposite view, and all nations
would hasten at the first signal of the adoption
of such views, to exterminate such open treason to God and man.

This very position is now assumed by extreme secessionists.   Acknowledging at the
same time the validity of all the past action
of the Federal Government, most of which in
its nature endures forever, thereby admitting,
of necessity, the manifest, essential perpetuity

of the Union and Government, in the same
breath, with admirable consistency, they claim
that, by reason of some sudden and strange
discovery, henceforth this Union is no longer
perpetual, and, by the sublime fiat of South
Carolina, it is dissolved, and all foreign treaties and contracts with the United States are
ipso facto dissolved, and glory in their self-
elected position, only to be paralleled by that
of Algerine pirates !   Is such outrageous non-
sense to be received by any sober mind ?   The
cardinal essence of all Government is perpetuity.   Without it, there is no government.

By the constitutional provisions, the right
of indefinite amendment is on the one hand
secured ; a supreme judicial tribunal always
open to settle all controversies on the construc-
tion or effect of its provisions and the laws of
Congress ; with full representation both of
State and people, making and amending all
their laws ; and, on the other hand, by its
tenth article, vests forever in the Federal
Government exclusively, all its granted powers and such as are essential to their exercise,

which include the most complete array of sovereign power ever vested in any Constitutional Government, and reserves all other powers " to the States " respectively, " or to the people."

In the words of Washington in 1796 : " The basis of our political systems is the right of the people to make and alter their constitutions of government ; *but the Constitution, which at any time exists till changed by an explicit and authentic act of the whole people, is sacredly obligatory upon all. The very idea of the power* and the *right* of the people to *establish* government, *presupposes the duty of every individual* to *obey the established government.*"

If the legislative, judicial, and executive *powers* of the *Constitution* and the Union, by their express grants, *extend* to and are to be *enforced upon every person* residing in the Union, irrespective of and *paramount to all State-laws and powers*, and by the admission of the secessionists, *have been* thus *rightfully* exercised *since* 1789, of what effect in sober common sense, not to speak of laws or Constitution, is the act of secession, by any

State, or by all the People of any one or more
States, upon the perpetuity of the Constitution and Union ? One effect only, viz. : to
strengthen the patriotic attachment of all loyal
citizens to the Union, confirm its perpetuity,
and enforce the penalties of treason by the
whole federal strength, and the unanimous
voluntary aid of all Union-loving citizens,
south and north.

If the Federal Government will do its duty
as required by the Constitution, and enforce
its supreme authority over all the people, the
flimsy shelter that no power is granted to coerce a State into obedience, disappears at the
first shot. The Union and the Government
bears on every person, and the State Governments, merely of municipal and police subordinate powers, disappear from the issue.

Without exhausting our subject, we have
said enough for our argument on the abstract
question.

At some seasons, and it may be now, it is
necessary to put in clear light the essential nature of our political system. Its simple state-

ment refutes every pretext of disloyalty ; and above all is it essential, when treason shows its horrid front in high places, and with loud pretensions claims support from and seeks to mislead some of our brethren.

We will close this paper, by again quoting the words of Washington in 1796, in his final appeal to his countrymen for all time :

" The unity of government, which constitutes you one people, is also now dear to you. It is justly so : for it is a main pillar in the edifice of your real independence—the support of your tranquility at home, your peace abroad, of your safety, of your prosperity, of that very liberty which you so highly prize. But as it is easy to foresee, that from different causes and from different quarters, much pains will be taken, many artifices employed, to weaken in your minds the conviction of this truth ; as this is the point in your political fortress against which the batteries of internal and external enemies will be most constantly and actively (though often covertly and insidiously) directed—it is of infinite moment that you should properly estimate the immense value of your national Union to your collective and individual happiness, that you should cherish a cordial, habitual, and immovable attachment to it; accustoming yourselves to think and speak of it as the palladium of your political safety and prosperity, watching for its preservation with jealous anxiety, discountenancing whatever may suggest even a suspicion that it can in any event be abandoned, and *indignantly frowning upon the first dawning of every attempt to alienate any portion of our country from the rest, or to enfeeble the sacred ties which now link together the various parts.*"

RODOLPHUS.

February, 27th 1861.

3

III.

THE QUESTION OF THE DAY.

It is plain from what has been already said, that Secession will not bear the daylight of reason, common sense, law, or Constitution, in argument on abstract grounds ; and that it is also the very evil and danger which Washington forewarned his children against for all time.

But say the secessionists, in the words of Howell Cobb, at Montgomery, Ala. : "Secession is an accomplished fact, argue as you may. We are out of the Union, and by our own inherent sovereign rights, have formed and now ordain a new Southern Confederacy, and claim recognition as an independent Government."

The Federal Government cannot without suicide, and never will, acknowledge this Southern Confederacy. In their eyes and before the law and Constitution, this Confederacy is an organized insurrection ; and every person adhering to these enemies is within the definition and penalties of treason. If thus considered by the Federal Government, representing all the rest of the nation, no civilized government, in alliance with the United States, which includes all the powers of the world, can, without breaking treaties, law of nations, and declaring war against the Union, in any way recognize their existence, either *de facto* or *de jure*. Unbroken peace and commerce with the United States, is the cardinal aim and interest of all our allies. The victories in Mexico raised us at once before Europe, as one of the most formidable military powers ; and the conquests of our diplomacy, with our social, inventive, and national progress and growth, rank us as a great power of the world, enthroned in a boundless empire, with illimitable resources, by which alone the old world

can sustain their existence. Is it conceivable
for a n.oment, that the older powers will, for
any price whatever, exchange, as they must,
all their old and profitable alliances with the
present Union, and substitute a flimsy bargain
with a sand-rope of a mere confederacy at
pleasure, of a few revolted subjects of the
Union ?

The official journals in Paris and London
have already conclusively answered the South
on this question, by an unconditional and in-
dignant refusal.   By these frank and full statements from official quarters, we read with
shame and surprise that Americans—children
of Washington's hope and faith—have been
long since so lost to all patriotism, as, under
the disguise of agents of Southern commercial
conventions, to visit European courts, with
offers to sell their birthright as Americans, for
the mess of pottage of foreign alliance with
themselves, in hostility to the Constitution and
Union.   They have fawned and eaten dirt before the French emperor in vain ; for even
this great modern usurper, endowed with con-

summate sagacity, has turned his back on them in well-deserved contempt.

We think that it has been demonstrated that Secession is legally impossible, and that the Union remains forever—a perpetual obligation on all citizens ; and that the remedy for all overt acts, besides paper resolutions and speeches, is plainly defined by the Constitution and laws of the government of the Union. We do not mean to be understood as advising at once the march of armies, or to open the Pandora box of civil war. However plain in principle and fact the iniquity may be, as we said at the beginning, the Union is strong enough to await in calm readiness for the re-turning common sense of our seceding brethren, to dissolve the airy fabrics of their vanity and wounded political ambition, and bring them voluntarily into the even tenor of duty to the Union.

We believe that all these violent measures are the work of exasperated and defeated poli-ticians ; that the conventions have been made unanimous by terrorism, preventing the free-
3*

dom of the polls or ballot or opinion, and that the conservative people have neither voted, spoken or been heard in this tumult, but are yet to speak out in tones of thunder. We believe that when their proceedings are sought to be changed from paper to practice, and these Southern people sought to be driven out of peace and safety into political suicide and annihilation by literal compliance, the whole sober, conservative body of that people will either emigrate at once, or, by open resistance, overthrow the demagogues and their work, and restore the reign of the Constitution and the Union ; or, if unsuccessful, inaugurate an endless and fatal civil war ; under which this Southern Confederacy will sink to its natural and speedy ruin, without the necessity of foreign invasion, now imminent from all quarters.

By seceding, if we are to understand them to be in earnest, they voluntarily and absolutely surrender all right to any Federal property whatsoever. There is no *locus pœnitentiæ*. They cannot, on their own theory, first secede, and next, when independent and separate, claim any division of property with us. We never were partners. All Federal property always has been and will be exclusive. There can be no shares. We all, over seventy years since, surrendered all such rights or claims forever. But even admitting such a claim, we answer that we refuse to dissolve the Union on any terms. We are the vast majority, and if you choose to consider the Union a mere voluntary society of States, as such majority we rightfully claim, hold, own, and must retain, all Federal property, all alliances and all interests of every nature, and which property we shall take good care of, and prevent all interference by you or any other "foreign power."

The *ultimate* basis of all financial and banking credit in each of the States has long been the security of the federal stocks, or, in other words, the Federal Government. Always at a premium in later years, they have been sought for and relied upon at home and abroad as the highest form of security for investment, upon whose basis corporations of all kinds, of the largest capital and designs, have been created and are in successful career. On secession theories, (but herein we know they are not sincere enough to carry them out,) the federal stocks are at once destroyed and repudiated, and, in their place, they expect shrewd practical men to accept the shinplasters of a Southern Confederacy, embodying every element of dissolution, without a treasury or revenue— as free trade is to be sovereign — or the slightest prospect or means of redemption, whilst, unless they also repudiate, they are now already immensely indebted, so that the interest alone of their general indebtedness is an annual sum far beyond all possible resources, and they seek still further to incur enormous debt, by assuming all the expenses of a government, army, and navy, with its enormous expense. ˙Credit is impossible on their own theory.

Another immediate barrier lies in the path of Secession by any State which did not form one of the thirteen original British Colonies,

who, as the United States of America, forming
one Government, were, by the treaty of peace
with Great Britain, recognized as an independent, united, sovereign government, and absolute proprietor of all the domain once owned
by the crown or lord proprietors or charter-
ers on this continent. By success in the war
of independence they succeeded to all such
rights, but only in their Federal Union or
capacity of united government. No treaty
ever recognized any such rights in the respective States. From the era of the Declaration
of Independence we have ever, as a nation and
government, been united under a federal head,
imperfectly under the Confederation, but con-
solidated by the Constitution.

In the case of Georgia or South Carolina,
then, two of the original thirteen, on their
own theory of Secession, they abandon forever
all benefit and rights under this treaty, to
which the Union alone was a party, and must
revert in their isolation to their original condition in 1775, weak, dependent, revolted British
colonies, usurping property and privileges

never granted, and throwing away as useless
all the blood and treasure of the Revolution,
with its thousand heroic memories, besides
every other substantial acquisition of the Union
which, since that early period, not yet a century, has, with the step of a young giant,
crossed to the Pacific and into the plains of
Mexico, and holds within its beneficent ægis a
mighty continent. The other four States,
Louisiana, Mississippi, Alabama, Florida—if
Texas is not included, to which also the same
argument applies—were each purchased by the
Federal Government from the Federal treasury and the revenues of the Union, although
by the laws of Congress each was admitted on
the same footing as the original States, by the
same law in each case, all laws of the United
States were made paramount and of the same
force within each of such new States. The
absolute sovereignty of the Union, under the
Constitution, *was expressly reserved* by their
creation ; and the political question is now
offered by them to the rest of the Union,
whether they will permit these States to rob

them, in open day, of acquisitions of such enormous cost ? Such an issue is already answered.

Another interest of vast importance—the free navigation and proprietorship of the Mississippi, Missouri, and their tributaries, with all the commerce of the mighty West and Northwest to the Rocky Mountains—is involved. This was an express condition of the admission of Louisiana by the Act of 1812, 8th April. She accepted her State existence on that condition and agreement with the Union. *Can her secession* repeal it ? There were *two parties* to that special condition. Can any one believe that all that immense region, now the dominant power in the Union, and destined always so to remain, whose commerce depends on this free navigation, will quietly submit to the creation of an independent proprietary government, holding exclusive possession of its great outlet to the Gulf of Mexico ? The Union is, above all, their first security of existence ; and no one can imagine that they are ready to accept in its stead the flimsy resolutions of any confederacy, dissolvable at pleasure, whilst retaining possession of the main artery of their life. On this topic far more might well be said ; but we think enough appears to show Secession impracticable.

The candid inquirer justly asks, What is the occasion of all these secession proceedings ? —what is the cause of this quarrel ? Have all the Union and the Federal Government deprived these seceding citizens of any of their rights ? We look into the Constitution and find that the Federal Government has never had the power so to do ; and its history shows the direct reverse. Has any such wrong been done by the people of the other States ? We find that in many of those States the people, the only sovereigns everywhere, have abolished slavery within their own respective States, and have sometimes enacted, that whatever slave should touch their soil, as in England, should thereby become free. Their sovereign right and power so to enact cannot, on secession theories, be questioned. By withdrawing from the Union and pretending to be a foreign government, they absolutely *concede* this right, the same as any other internal regulation of foreign governments. But the question of the validity of such laws is at this moment on the calendar for argument in the Lemmon case before the Supreme Court of the Union, whose decision will, to all loyal citizens, be final. Seceders profess to repudiate this tribunal, with all their rights under the Constitution and the Union, and all peaceable adjustment, and substitute open war.

We also find that in some of the States the popular sentiment, irritated both by Southern menace and outrage of person and opinion, and also by the false doctrines and clamor of the Abolitionists, have enacted laws which prevent the enforcement by their citizens of the Fugitive Slave Laws of Congress. By the plain words of the Constitution, such enactments are *merely void*, and will readily be so declared by the competent tribunal. Some of these States have already in advance repealed such laws, and although they have been long existing in these States, practically, as has been fully shown, they are a dead letter. The supreme authority

4

of the Union and its laws is acknowledged in
all States, and fugitive slaves are restored to
their owners by virtue thereof, regardless of
such State laws and penalties. On the other
hand, have we ever complained and sought dissolution of the Union because the South claim
absolute property in their slaves within their
States, or tar and feather and, by lawless mobs,
murder abolition missionaries, or any Northern
man whose political opinions do not suit their
own, or punish as a crime the instruction of
slaves, or because the slaveholding States have,
from the beginning until now, sometimes mo-
nopolized the Federal offices and patronage?
Recrimination has not been the fault of the
other States; on the contrary, the extreme
South has always boastingly relied on their
quiet submission. The peaceful remedy of the
ballot has effected a revolution in political history. The Northwestern free States have *first
achieved* this utter demolition of the political
ambition of these secessionist politicians.
They have themselves alone to thank for it.
With the power in their hands, they wilfully

broke with their Democratic Northern friends from the North at Charleston and Baltimore, threw away their party, its candidates, offices, and future, and surrendered, in their quarrel, to the political enemy, who was thus triumphantly elected by their divisions ; whilst, for all this century, whenever united, the Democratic party has been and is the undisputed owner of place and power in the nation.

But openly in Congress, say their leaders, this regular constitutional election of Lincoln to the restricted powers of the Constitution is *not the cause* of our sudden secession and extreme haste to try, by all expedients, to get out of the Union and the power of his adherents, before the 4th of March, 1861. However inconsistent, we must accept their own words, and if so, we almost preclude further inquiry for any substantial ground. But we will ask, is it because the Chicago platform, besides the customary party promises, declared open hostility to the introduction of slavery in the public domain ? Can any one peruse the Dred Scott decision and not be satisfied that such a declaration is directly opposite to the supreme law of the land, and therefore any attempt by law of Congress for such end is absolutely void ? The Constitution, as thus settled, *prohibits* such legislation.

Since that decision, and certainly the highest evidence that these secessionists felt of themselves their security to be in the Constitution and the Union, the recorded vote of their senators in the United States Senate, only in May, 1860, in a majority of 43 to 5, carried a resolution, submitted by Mr. Clingman, of North Carolina, " That the existing condition of the Territories of the United States *does not require* the intervention of Congress for the protection of " property in slaves." This majority—almost an unanimity—of the senators who established this record, included the senators of all those seceding States, who have lately, within less than a year since, outraged all senatorial decorum and patriotism, by flourishing valedictories in the Senate. Further comment is needless.

We need not say that, so far from there

being any real danger to the slave-owner within
his State, in the Union, its whole power is
pledged for his protection ; but dissolve the
Union, if it were possible, and they themselves
stab slavery to the heart ; and can any reflec-
tive mind fail to perceive that the existence of
slavery in any of the public Territories is not
the subject of law of Congress, but is *only
dependent* on the *divine laws* of climate, soil,
situation, and products ? On cereal land,
slavery, however jealously forced and strength-
ened, cannot, as all experience shows, perma-
nently exist ; and at all times, when new
States are to be formed from the residents of
present Territory, on the principle of the Kan-
sas bill, the question of its existence is to be de-
cided by the territorial people themselves alone.
But, driven to their last corner in argument,
say the secessionists, we dissolve the Union to
escape the hostile public opinion of the North
against us and our slavery ! This remedy is
far worse than the disease ; it is taking yellow
fever to cure dyspepsia—voluntary suicide ;
inviting on their own devoted heads all the ig-
4*

nominy of their treason, the whole military and
naval power of the Union and the world ; all
possible prohibitory tariffs and blockades ; all
manner of political, social, and private ruin
and disgrace, as the result of skulking, like
cowards, from free discussion in Congress or the
Supreme Court, on equal terms in the Union,
or stifling by bluster, the appeals of conscience
and reason ;—and all this, because, in this land
and age of free public opinion, the great majority of the Union and of all mankind, see fit
to differ with them on the *abstract and purely
moral question* of the right or expediency of
slavery.   Does not such a course out-Herod
the Herod of Abolitionism ?   Does it not
stimulate to over-weening triumph the whole
brood of Abolition ?   Is it not total surrender
and defeat ?

But, as if to render all search for motives
impossible, their Southern Confederacy, so
called, in process of incubation, *adopts*, with a
prohibition of the slave trade and any obstruc-
tion of the Mississippi, *the whole present Constitution of the Union !*   By this act, secession

itself has committed suicide ; the people, obey-
ing the same laws and government in effect,
return or *remain in the Union*, by whatever
pretext or designation the Constitution may
bear in the words of politicians. They thereby
concede and reëstablish solemnly the fact, that
the Constitution of the United States is the
most perfect of all human governments. The
frame-work, like mere scaffolding, of Southern
Confederacy, will, we trust, shortly fall away
from the noble edifice, and our Southern brethren thus, by their own action, return to reason
and allegiance.

We have forborne to say another word on
the deep conviction of the community. The
proofs are not fully developed ; but no one,
familiar with current events, can doubt that the
secession movement is but an organized con
spiracy by its leaders, defeated in the late elec
tion, to win renewed place and power over their
misguided and rash Southern supporters ; and,
that from the era of the disorganization of
the Democratic party, it has been deeply laid,

fostered by the public plunder and connivance
of recreants in the Cabinet and office, and
nursed into its present proportions by the
weakness, to use no other terms, of the President. Spirit of Washington and Jackson, de-
fend that this be really so !

Whether this be so or not, what is the remedy ? is the more important question. The
secessionists, by their own act of adoption of
the Constitution, give their own answer, echoed
back by a large portion of the Union. The
secessionists are solemnly requested to declare
their grievances in Congress ; they repudiate
this obvious preliminary to all negotiation, and
reject *in limine* all proffers of compromise. If
this be the sober sentiment of their people, our
only remedy and strength is to sit still under
the Constitution and laws of the Union, and
let their frenzy run its brief career.

But we are unwilling to believe them to be
beyond all accommodation. Without war—
without aggression—or any form of forcible
coercion, which are remote from the wishes of

the Union at large—however they may be threatened by fanatical prints, the laws of the land are the peaceable and most effectual means now in hand of bringing back our erring brethren. We have thus far proved our forbearance at many robberies of federal property and shameless insults of the federal power ; any of which were felt by the aggressors to be just cause of war.

In return, we find Congress submitting and debating propositions for accommodation and settlement, and in the Capitol, at the same time, propositions and offers of a like purport are preparing, by a convention of the delegates from twenty States—free and slaveholding— nearly all the rest of the Union. The secessionists refuse to be present in either body, or to state there any grievances ; but on all hands the olive branch of peaceful settlement is preparing. When these proposals are matured and offered, no doubt in another week, and before the ashes are gathered over this dying Administration, it will be proper to discuss their

merits ; at present it would depart from the
object of these papers as stated in their outset.

RODOLPHUS.

March 6, 1861.

IV.

OUR CIVIL WAR.

From the year 1789, the inauguration of the Government of the Union under the Constitution, to the present day not a year has elapsed in which the great powers of the world have not waged war, either with revolution in their own states, or with foreign enemies. These wars and revolutions have surpassed all history in their sanguinary and gigantic character.

This period of seventy-two years, which English and American writers expatiate upon, as the era of wonderful progress of arts and civilization, equals in the number of its wars, and far surpasses in their magnitude, all the records of the past.

No one, in the least familiar with its history,

can doubt this ; nor that the supreme energies of civilized man, throughout this period of the highest civilization, have been given to war, which has carried on its fiery chariot-wheels all the arts, skill, and science of mankind.

In previous centuries, history proves only an endless catalogue of battles and sieges ; and in such history the republics of the world may claim the pre-eminence.

War is, then, the normal, primary condition of civilized man, as with the savage ; the only difference is that civilized war is vastly more sanguinary and devastating.

Peace is accidental and temporary ; local, and never general.

Since we became a nation, although divinely harbored, on this distant continent, away from European collisions—in this brief period, which we are apt to call unbroken peace, we have had since 1789, besides our Revolutionary War,—our arming against France, our second war with England, war with Algiers and with Mexico as foreign foes, and diplomatic ruptures with Spain, England, France, and other powers ; this government has been called on to suppress organized treason in no less than eight different and successive forms ; besides constantly waging war, on a vast scale, on our frontiers, with the Indians and the Mormons.

For such a nation, from its infancy with every inducement to remain at peace, our own brief history confirms the position, that humanity, under the freest and highest form of government and culture—like the savage, and far worse—pursues the same primary and normal rule of war.

Such is the truth of history—sacred and secular. We believe fully in a Divine, Omniscient, Omnipresent, Ever-guiding Providence.

We believe that He is the same eternal power that led out the millions of Israel from Egypt, with a strong hand and a mighty arm ; that established, in his own theocracy of the Jews, with whom he visibly dwelt for so many ages, and to whom he gave the hopes of mankind, a thoroughly organized standing army, with orders to march forward to the conquest,

5

slaughter, and utter devastation, of all the
surrounding nations ; who blessed them for
their warlike valor and patriotism, and cursed
them for peaceful compromise of truth ; and
who made and recorded their whole history,
till its last hour, when it expired in blood and
flame at Jerusalem, one endless battle-field.
Israel was his peculiar people, whom he de-
lighted to honor.

The New Testament from heaven, heralded
by the angels as peace on earth, goodwill to
men, came first to the Jews, and through
them was carried to other nations. It is ad-
dressed to the same humanity, by the same
God. Whilst it blesses the peacemaker, and
attributes war to the evil passions of man, and
preaches the doctrines of forgiveness of injur-
ies, of mercy, and charity,—with its future
rewards and spiritual system, it enjoins on its
followers to render to Cæsar the things that
are Cæsar's ; to honor the king or supreme
governor ; to obey all magistrates and those in
authority ; to diligently and contentedly pursue their calling, whether soldier or citizen, in

God's fear ; and to remember that the magistrate doth .not bear the sword in vain,—while thus enjoining entire loyalty to existing and rightful authority and law, it leaves its disciples entirely free in all their civil relations ; its kingdom not of this world ; its disciples lambs among wolves ; it recognizes the same normal condition of humanity—war, in all the ages, until the Millenium.

He that disobeys the patriot summons to war is no Christian, and unworthy to enjoy the blessing of peace.

In our century thus far, the fruits of war have been progress in civilization and freedom.

Take man as he is, and always has been, and, instead of dilating on the alleged barbarism of war, we must admit that Providence has thus far permitted it as the great agent of progress.

But the glorious and enthusiastic rally of the loyal and patriotic States, at the call of the President, dispenses with any need of abstract speculation.

The infamous assault on eighty men at

Sumter, by ten thousand of the Southern chivalry of treason, followed by even the more infamous proclamation of Jefferson Davis, inviting the pirates of the South to prey on our shipping, and their infamous boast that Washington will be in their hands in less than sixty days, has proved a louder tocsin than the news of Bunker Hill.

The lightning flashed it north, east, and west ; not a week has elapsed, and already, instead of only 75,000 men, a million has buckled on its armor, and ready, nay crowding, to get at this crew of Algerine corsairs of the sea and land.

A hundred millions of money from this city alone is now ready and offered to the government, as much and perhaps more from other cities and sections ; and million after million of men, with countless shipping, are ready at call. At this hour of our history we are above all politics and parties. We have ceased to discuss the specious falsehoods of Secession ; they have declared war against the most benignant government that ever blessed mankind, which from the very outset of the rebellion for the last weary five months and more, has with forbearing magnanimity submitted to every outrage at their hands, and in every form tendered to these shameless traitors the olive branch of peace. They now throw down the gauntlet of open piracy, slave trade, and war.

They have thus invited on their devoted heads all the ignominy of their treason, the whole military and naval power of the Union and the world, all prohibitory tariffs and blockades and devastation, all manner of political, social, and private ruin and disgrace ; and all this as the result of skulking as coward traitors from free discussion in Congress or the Supreme Court, on equal terms in the Union, or stifling by bluster the voice of conscience and reason ; and declare war and piracy, because, in this land and age of free opinion and free speech, the vast majority of the Union and all mankind see fit to differ with them on the right or expediency of slavery, and its expansion beyond their borders.

5*

Spirit of Washington ! was ever a cause more worthy of your patriot zeal ?

We feel that we speak the sentiment of the loyal Union.

Let this war, now forced upon us, be speedy, overwhelming to extermination. Nothing but the most thorough triumph and destruction is adapted to the crisis. Let us have no delays, no Florida campaign of endless length. With brave men in nations, and money in countless millions, and all civilized nations as our allies, this contest should be short, and as destructive as the fiercest traitor of the South can desire.

Who can doubt the result ? Who can fail to see the fleeing slaves, and the uprising Union men of the South, joining our forces for the destruction of these self-elected traitor demagogues ?

Let the war be long or short, the Union is fully ready ; and with the war comes universal relief from suspense, and, into all commercial countries, reviving commerce and affluence.

NEW YORK, *April* 18, 1861.

V.

THE SUBJUGATION.

THE rebel traitors to God and man, of the South, affect to despise the power of this government and to rally their courage by asserting that it is impossible *to subjugate the South*, however numerous and great may be our conquests ; they will make all their swamp-coasts, and border, fastnesses for defence, and rallying points for new armies, to wage a ceaseless guerilla warfare ; and with shameless insolence they pretend to be the successors of our patriot sires, and waging a Revolutionary war on their own soil for the defence of their homes and altars.

Our purpose is to show that *subjugation* of the South—complete and entire—is *inevitable*.

The Roman empire was created and main-

tained by its army. By the Testament of
Augustus, its boundaries were fixed on the
north at the wall of Agricola, or near the
present line of the Caledonian canal, in Scotland, the Danube and Scythia, or modern Russia, on the continent ; on the west by the Atlantic Ocean ; on the south, by the African
desert ; and on the east, by the Euphrates.
These limits were only once altered by his
successors ; in the conquest of Dacia, by Tra-
jan, which carried the north-eastern boundary
into Scythia—up to the river Dniester.

Until the middle of the eighteenth century
this vast area comprised the whole civilized
portion of the old world, and with some exception, it does so still.

According to the accurate research of Gibbon, the aggregate population of the Roman
empire, or as the Gospel names it, "*the whole
world,*" in the time of the Emperor Claudius,
about the era of the outset of its wondrous
career, was one hundred and twenty millions
of souls, of whom fairly two thirds were barbarian tribes ; many of which, as in Britain and

Germany, on the authority of Tacitus, were of the most warlike character ; of these, Britain alone contained fifty tribes, who twice repulsed the legions of Cæsar, and whose strength only yielded after a century of warfare ; while Germany swarmed with numerous savage nations, against whom the fortified camps on the Danube alone protected the empire, until overborne by the masses of the Goths and Huns.

By the ratios of modern census, during about two hundred years from the accession of Augustus, in which Rome held peaceful and undisputed sway over the world, unbroken by foreign wars of magnitude, its population must have between two hundred and two hundred and fifty millions of souls.

The highest computation of its entire army and navy, at the maximum of its strength and grandeur, is fixed by Gibbon at not to exceed four hundred and fifty thousand men.

Their slaves, a vast multitude, do not appear to be computed in their estimate of population, and of course were not in their army.

It is impossible to estimate their number; the data are wanting; some wealthy Romans are stated to have owned twenty thousand: on such a basis all that can be estimated is a vast indefinite multitude to be added to the aggregate of population returns, whilst it proved a source of weakness and self-destruction to the empire.

A Legion—with all its auxiliaries, then, was formed of twelve thousand five hundred men.

The entire maximum average military and naval strength required to *subjugate the whole civilized world*, and which kept it in unbroken peaceful submission to Rome for near two centuries, and would have continued to maintain its subjection, and the unity of the empire, but for its own internal corruption—was but thirty-six legions in number at the outside, or four hundred and fifty thousand, against two hundred millions of barbarians exclusive of the numerous millions of slaves.

By our modern conscriptions fifteen millions of Romans were subject to military duty.

When we add to these results the fact that

all these legions, with the exception of the Pretorians, were posted in their fortified camps, in the heart of their conquests ; at great distances from Rome, never in cities ; that the military roads, with their six-mile posts and relays, traversed the empire, from all its legions to Rome, its centre, we see that numerical strength of armies is not the only means of subjugation.

The discipline of the Roman legions and the terror of their eagles were not enough to subdue the fierce barbarians. Germany, Gaul, and Britain long resisted with success. The weapons of the Roman army were often unequal to those of their enemies. Surrounding and supporting the legion were the Roman laws and civilization; and municipal institutions grew on the sites and vicinity of their camps, with free toleration of religion. In the lapse of generations their humanizing influence subdued the wild barbarian, and made the privilege of Roman citizenship of the highest value to the descendants of those who hated the name of Rome. Saul of Tarsus and Constantine of Britain. alike, with countless others, are examples.

From the era of the Antonines till the conquest of Byzantium by the Turks in 1453,
through all those twelve centuries of corruption
in its government, of weakness, decline, and
fall, its military strength in numbers never ap-
proached the above, but steadily diminished.

This aggregate of the military strength of
Rome has been immensely surpassed by single
nations, once their provinces, in modern history,
—France under Louis XIV., and again by Napoleon, for the invasion of Russia. The coali-
tion of England and Germany in 1815 against
Napoleon placed a million in arms, besides the
vast navy that held all the seas against France ;
and the united naval and military strength of
the allies before Sebastopol, exceeded that of
Rome.

The present regular army of France, exclusive of its navy, comprises five hundred thousand men ; that of England exceeds three
hundred thousand men, besides its fleets.

The present entire population of France is
about thirty-seven millions, with a government
at peace, although revolutionary and aggres-

sive in its diplomacy, as yet without foreign or domestic war.

The present standing armies and navies of Europe combine an aggregate of nearly four millions of men ; and this vast number, yearly increasing, is now required by these governments to hold in peace the same area of empire which Rome held in subjection with less than half a million, as well as thereby extended its power in Asia.

Such is the result, notwithstanding the vast superiority of modern arms, securing, as we are told, the great reduction of combatants ; and also the great advance and extent of modern civilization.

Surely, the Roman legionary in his helmet and mail, with his buckler, sword, and pike, and severe discipline, through all the ages before artillery, must have been a far superior power to the modern soldier, armed with all the results of science and civilization ; and the Roman empire, with all its corruptions, must have been of vastly greater strength than all or any of its modern successors.

6

Familiar from childhood with the exploits of the Roman legions, many of us are apt to imagine the legionary to have been of gigantic stature and strength.

In the Museo Borbonico, at Naples, saved by the ashes from Vesuvius, is the skeleton and armor of the last of the Romans of the age of Titus. He is a legionary, who stood guard at the gate of Pompeii, at the time of its destruction.

A modern of six feet stature and average proportions, would find his armor nearly a foot too small. He would have been rejected by Frederick of Prussia and Napoleon, and would scarcely be accepted for the poorest infantry of modern times.

Of the military strength of Greece we have no accurate data. It could not have been very great. Its wars of history were of internal revolution or defence, not of foreign conquest.

It is curious, however, to note in this connection, that whilst all the rest of Greece retained the phalanx of sixteen thousand men fighting eighteen deep in close array, Sparta divided its army into " *morai*" or regiments, commanded by colonels and lieutenants—the size of its regiments varying from one thousand to two hundred and fifty men ; and that their uniform was *scarlet* by the law of Lycurgus, whose reason for that color was that it would not show the stain of blood.

From Sparta, therefore, we derive the modern regiment with its officers, and the scarlet uniform of England, which first achieved its victories on the Ironsides of Cromwell at Marsten Moor, and has since encircled the globe with its valor.

In 1776 the whole population of the original thirteen United States—New Hampshire to Georgia—the Atlantic border, was 2,616,300 souls.

In 1800 it was 5,300,000 in all.

In 1815 it was about 8,000,000 in all.

In 1860, of our present 32,000,000—against less than eight millions of whites in all, in the slave States, are twenty millions in the free States, besides four millions of slaves. During the seven years' war of the Revolution, in all two hundred thousand men enlisted in our Continental army, averaging between twenty and thirty thousand men annually.

Our second war with Great Britain was fought by far less than one hundred thousand ; its crowning victories were by sea and on the lakes, although our army won imperishable laurels, amidst western treachery and disgrace, on our northern frontier and at New Orleans.

The Mexican war, conquering a vast territory and nation, of far more numerous armies, led by brave men of military skill, was fought by the masterly genius of Taylor and Scott, with less than thirty thousand men.

All these wars of our history were waged to triumph against vast odds. We conquered the overwhelming military superiority of England—the terror of the world—the conquerors Waterloo, and whose advance was sustained by tories and traitors throughout the country, at the period of our greatest weakness, a feeble handful of people, without money, army, with little more than our patriot courage, guided by

Washington, Franklin, and their glorious associates and successors.

The civil war in England, 1642–1651, during which its entire population averaged four millions of souls, may furnish some data, and to some minds an analogy in the great issues involved in the struggle ; less than one hundred thousand men in all, on both sides, waged this whole war. Fifty thousand soldiers, under Cromwell, utterly subjugated England, Scotland, and Ireland, king and parliaments.

More complete mastery was never attained ; and no period in English history can surpass the union and loyalty of all classes to the government founded by Cromwell on the victories of his army.

It was *not* the *subjection of the conquered,* ready to revolt, on the removal of the army. On the peace the whole army was disbanded and returned to civil life ; and instead of being lawless banditti, they all resumed their former civil industry, and became as eminent in the walks of private and social duty as they had been in the field. The government had

6*

no longer any need of its army ; it was strong
enough in the respect and loyalty of its subjects ; no standing army was required or maintained.

So it will be, as it has always been with us,
a few victorious fields of battle, and the whole
South is at our feet begging for mercy.

The soldiers of Cromwell were his own
selection ; they were the sons of respectable
farmers, citizens, and mechanics ; industrious,
moral, patriotic, and with strong interest in the
soil, and its government. Cromwell gathered
his army in 1644, two years after the first battle of Edgehill. Lord Essex commanded during these two years, for the Parliament, men,
as Cromwell said, far inferior to the Royal
forces ; " tapsters, serving men, and fellows of
the meaner sort," and with such troops could
never trust them in action or pursuit. The
king constantly gained in strength, and in two
years held three-fourths of the kingdom.

Cromwell drilled his new levies to the se-
verest rule, fired their zeal by the chaplains
and his personal address. They passed prepar-

atory months in drilling, preaching, and pray-
ing ; and at their first appearance in battle—
Marston Moor—they were found not only in-
vincible, but swept the splendid army of cava-
lier aristocracy to destruction ; and thenceforth
marched on conquering and to conquer, never
beaten, never checked, nothing could withstand
them. The terror of their prowess is immortal
yet.

Of the same material, in general, is our
army composed, and with like drill and moral
discipline. With the ablest living soldier at
their head, what hinders their like career of
conquest ? Who are the foes ? Except in
contradictory newspaper statements we know
little of them. We find no army, no organi-
zation, few arms, no money, and what is worse,
no cause to fight for, save the ambition of their
leaders. The poorest whites—" mud-sills " as
they call them—are forced into the ranks.

The self-styled aristocracy must all .be
officers ; and without commissariat, with general drunkenness and lack of all moral discipline or drill, however some may abound in

courage, the whole army is at the outset thoroughly demoralized and disabled.

Traitors and thieves never fight as armies; a few desperate leaders may; but bluster and bravado, in which they are all so proficient, are the surest proofs of cowardice.

Contrast this with the calm, earnest, united, determined, universal arming of the loyal States. In less than six weeks, out of the ground, as it were, sprang up two hundred thousand men, ready armed; farmers, mechanics, merchants, with patriot interest in the Union, of thorough drill, completely equipped, and supplied with an overflowing treasury, a vast fleet, with endless resources in reserve, the navy, the government, and alliance of the world,—with capable leaders, who does not see *utter subjugation* and entire victory for the glorious star-spangled banner that now, and has so often, led us in triumph over all our foes?

This great arming of the Union has no parallel in history. Napoleon, for the last great struggle of France against the world in arms,⁷ forcing all conscriptions with all the energy of despair in 1815, in two months and a half got together less than 150,000 men ; all he could raise to face their enemies in the Waterloo campaign ; and before that action, only 75,000 men, the flower of his army, veterans and marshals who had followed the eagles of that Alexander through all the battle-fields of Europe, alone remained to try the issue of dominion over Europe.

Not a volunteer was in his ranks. The English force was largely volunteer recruits.

But four years since, and all India, with its two hundred millions of souls, was in the power of the Sepoy rebels. A vast continent was suddenly seized from the British crown ; and the world sickened at the horrors of the Sepoys. They began, long before, their insidious arts and plans to seize all the government property, and banish all loyal officers and subjects ; it was a war of religion, treachery, and the uprising of all that is base in heathenism. For the first year it was a desperate struggle ; England seemed overmatched ; but 100,000

troops under skilful leaders conquered their
strongholds, and drove forth the rebels ; and
ever since their complete and sudden subjection has prevailed.

Our Indian mutiny has by *like acts* and
treachery culminated ; the disciplined valor of
the Union will sweep to destruction these
Southern Sepoys ; and they, with their flying
leaders, if they escape the hemp or bullet, will
seek their natural place of *buccaneers, Walker
fillibusters,* and soon gain the reward of all
other pirates.

The mighty Union sentiment of the Southern people, no longer subdued by terror, will
rise as suddenly and powerfully ; the slaves
will flee ; and, to their own surprise, a thorough social regeneration will begin. Northern
enterprise will buy their soil, and, with free
industry, will produce for the first time in their
history of constant decline, profitable returns ;
and the South, instead of depending solely on
the annual hazards of but one crop—cotton—
always produced by slaves at a loss, will, like

the North, enter the markets of the world in every field of industry and culture.

Great are the blessings already of this united patriotism of the Union ; but greater far will be its beneficent results to South and North.

New York, *May* 25, 1861.

LE Ja '13

A BOOK FOR EVERY SOLDIER'S KNAPSACK.

𝔗racts for the 𝔚ar.

SECESSION:

THE REMEDY AND RESULT.

NEW YORK:
PUBLISHED BY JAMES MILLER,
(SUCCESSOR TO C. S. FRANCIS & CO.,)
522 BROADWAY.
1861.

www.ingramcontent.com/pod-product-compliance
Lightning Source LLC
Chambersburg PA
CBHW020238090426
42735CB00010B/1744